THIS BOOK BELONGS TO:

_____

_____

Shop our other books at
www.sillyslothpress.com

For questions and customer service, email us at
support@sillyslothpress.com

JOKE 1

A CANNIBAL IS ON TRIAL. THE JUDGE ASKS WHAT THE DEFENDANT HAS TO SAY ABOUT HIS SENTENCE.

THE CANNIBAL REPLIES, "IF YOU ARE WHAT YOU EAT, THEN I AM THE TRUE VICTIM HERE!"

JOKE 2

Q: WHY IS IT COMMON FOR LAWYERS TO BE LOST IN THOUGHT?

A: UNFAMILIAR TERRITORY.

JOKE 3

Q: CAN YOU TELL ME THE DIFFERENCE BETWEEN A BAD LAWYER AND A GOOD LAWYER?

A: A BAD LAWYER WILL LET A CASE DRAG ON FOR YEARS. A GOOD LAWYER MAKES IT LAST EVEN LONGER!

JOKE 4

Q: HAVE YOU HEARD THAT THERE IS A NEW "DIVORCED" BARBIE DOLL?

A: SHE COMES WITH ALIMONY AND THE DREAMHOUSE.

JOKE 5

Q: HOW CAN YOU TELL THE DIFFERENCE BETWEEN A CATFISH AND AN ATTORNEY?

A: ONE IS A SCUM SUCKING BOTTOM FEEDER. THE OTHER IS A FISH.

JOKE 6

Q: HOW CAN YOU TELL THE DIFFERENCE BETWEEN A VACUUM CLEANER AND A LAWYER RIDING A MOTORCYCLE?

A: THE VACUUM HAS THE DIRT BAG ON THE INSIDE.

JOKE 7

Q: WHAT DO LAWYERS SAY DURING THEIR VOWS INSTEAD OF, "I DO"?

A: "I ACCEPT THE TERMS AND CONDITIONS."

JOKE 8

ATTORNEY: NOW THAT YOU HAVE BEEN FOUND NOT GUILTY, TELL ME THE TRUTH. DID YOU MURDER THAT PERSON?

CLIENT: AFTER HEARING YOUR ARGUMENTS, I'M BEGINNING TO BELIEVE I DIDN'T!

JOKE 9

ATTORNEY: MY CLIENT IS TRAPPED IN A PENNY!

JUDGE: EXCUSE ME?

ATTORNEY: HE'S IN-A-CENT

JOKE 10

Q: WHAT HAPPENS WHEN YOU CROSS AN ATTORNEY AND A LIBRARIAN?

A: ALL THE INFORMATION IN THE WORLD, BUT YOU CAN'T UNDERSTAND A WORD OF IT.

JOKE 11

Q: WHAT DO YOU GET WHEN YOU CROSS A POTBELLIED PIG AND A LAWYER?

A: NOTHING! THERE ARE SOME THINGS EVEN A PIG WON'T DO.

JOKE 12

Q: WHAT'S THE DIFFERENCE BETWEEN A VAMPIRE AND AN ATTORNEY?

A: VAMPIRES ONLY SUCK BLOOD AT NIGHT AND STOP WHEN THEY HAVE HAD THEIR FILL.

JOKE 13

"LAWYERS OCCASIONALLY STUMBLE OVER THE TRUTH, BUT MOST OF THEM PICK THEMSELVES UP AND HURRY OFF AS IF NOTHING HAD HAPPENED."

– WINSTON CHURCHILL

JOKE 14

Q: WHAT DOES THE BAILIFF HAVE FOR BREAKFAST?

A: OATHMEAL.

JOKE 15

Q: WHAT IS BROWN, STINKS, AND SITS IN A COURTROOM?

A: JURY DOODY.

JOKE 16

LAWYER PRO TIP: DON'T MAKE PLANS FOR THE DAY. THE WORD "PREMEDITATED" GETS THROWN AROUND A LOT IN THE COURTROOM.

JOKE 17

Q: WHY DON'T SHARKS ATTACK LAWYERS?

A: IT'S A MATTER OF PROFESSIONAL COURTESY.

JOKE 18

Q: WHAT'S THE DIFFERENCE BETWEEN A DIVORCE LAWYER AND A LEECH?

A: ONCE YOU'RE DEAD, A LEECH STOPS SUCKING YOUR BLOOD.

JOKE 19

Q: WHAT IS THE DIFFERENCE BETWEEN A TRAMPOLINE AND AN ATTORNEY?

A: YOU TAKE YOUR SHOES OFF BEFORE JUMPING ON A TRAMPOLINE.

JOKE 20

POLAROID FILED FOR BANKRUPTCY.

DETAILS TO COME AS THE STORY DEVELOPS.

JOKE 21

Q: WHY DID THE JUDGE DECLARE A RECESS WHEN THE LAWYER ARRIVED WITHOUT THE PROPER COURTROOM ATTIRE?

A: BECAUSE HE WASN'T WEARING HIS LAWSUIT!

JOKE 22

Q: WHO IS THE KIND, COURTEOUS, SOBER PERSON AT THE BAR ASSOCIATION ANNUAL CONVENTION?

A: THE CATERER.

JOKE 23

Q: HOW MANY ATTORNEYS DOES IT TAKE TO SCREW IN A LIGHTBULB?

A: THREE. ONE SCREWS IN THE BULB, THE OTHER WIGGLES THE LADDER, AND THE THIRD SUES THE LADDER COMPANY.

JOKE 24

Q: WHAT IS THE MOST COMMON FORM OF BIRTH CONTROL AMONGST LAWYERS?

A: THEIR PERSONALITIES.

JOKE 25

(A FATHER RUNS IN LATE TO PATERNITY COURT)

FATHER: I MADE IT!

JUDGE: EVIDENTLY, YOU DIDN'T.

JOKE 26

Q: CAN YOU NAME SOMETHING THAT NEVER WORKS WHEN IT'S FIXED?

A: A JURY.

Q: WHAT'S THE DIFFERENCE BETWEEN MY BIRTHDAY AND COURT?

A: MY DAD SHOWS UP TO COURT.

Q: HOW DO YOU KNOW WHEN A LAWYER IS TELLING LIE?

A: THEIR LIPS ARE MOVING.

JOKE 29

Q: WHAT IS A JUDGE'S FAVORITE DRINK?

A: GUILT-TEA.

JOKE 30

A LAWYER'S MANTRA: A CLIENT IS INNOCENT UNTIL PROVEN PENNILESS.

JOKE 31

Q: HOW CAN YOU TELL IF IT'S FREEZING COLD OUTSIDE?

A: LAWYERS HAVE THEIR HANDS IN THEIR OWN POCKETS.

JOKE 32

Q: CAN YOU TELL ME THE DIFFERENCE BETWEEN A TERRORIST AND A LAWYER?

A: YOU CAN NEGOTIATE WITH A TERRORIST.

JOKE 33

A PARTNER AT A LAW FIRM WAS ADMIRING HIS NEW OFFICE. SOMEONE KNOCKED ON HIS DOOR. TO IMPRESS THE POTENTIAL CLIENT, HE PICKED UP THE PHONE AND YELLED, "TWO MILLION DOLLARS, AND THAT'S MY FINAL OFFER!"

THE VOICE FROM BEHIND THE DOOR ENTERS AND SAYS, "I'M HERE TO HOOK UP YOUR PHONE".

JOKE 34

Q: WHY WAS THE COURTROOM ARTIST ARRESTED?

A: THE DETAILS ARE SKETCHY.

JOKE 35

Q: WHAT IS A FAVORITE GAME OF JUDGES?

A: COUNTER-STRIKE.

JOKE 36

Q: WHAT'S THE DIFFERENCE BETWEEN A LAWYER AND GOD?

A: GOD DOESN'T THINK HE'S A LAWYER.

JOKE 37

Q: HAVE YOU HEARD OF THE MAN WHO DIED AFTER THE JUDGE "THREW THE BOOK" AT HIM?

A: HE WAS SENTENCED TO DEATH.

JOKE 38

Q: WHY DID THE PROSTITUTE NOT GET CONVICTED OF MURDER?

A: BECAUSE THE JURY WAS HUNG.

JOKE 39

99% OF PERSONAL INJURY LAWYERS REALLY GIVE THE REST OF US A BAD NAME...

JOKE 40

Q: WHAT DO YOU GET IF YOU PUT A GROUP OF LAWYERS IN THE BASEMENT?

A: A WHINE CELLAR.

JOKE 41

Q: WHAT DO VACUUM CLEANERS AND LAWYERS HAVE IN COMMON?

A: THEY BOTH SUCK.

JOKE 42

Q: WHAT'S THE DIFFERENCE BETWEEN AN ATTORNEY AND A CPA?

A: CPAS KNOW THEY ARE BORING.

JOKE 43

Q: HOW DO LAWYERS SLEEP?

A: FIRST THEY LIE ON ONE SIDE, THEN THEY LIE ON THE OTHER.

JOKE 44

Q: WHAT DO YOU CALL A CASTRATED JUDGE?

A: JUSTICE PRICK.

JOKE 45

CLIENT: HOW MUCH DO YOU CHARGE FOR 3 QUESTIONS?

LAWYER: $500.00

CLIENT: ISN'T THAT A LITTLE PRICEY?

LAWYER: YEAH, IT IS....
SO, WHAT'S YOUR THIRD QUESTION?

JOKE 46

Q: WHAT DID THE JUDGE SAY WHEN THE SKUNK WAS BROUGHT INTO THE COURT ROOM?

A: ODOR IN THE COURT!

Q: WHAT HAPPENS WHEN YOU GIVE A LAWYER VIAGRA?

A: HE GETS TALLER.

Q: WHAT IS THE DIFFERENCE BETWEEN ROADKILL AND A DEAD ATTORNEY IN THE ROAD?

A: THERE ARE SKID MARKS IN FRONT OF THE ROADKILL.

JOKE 49

AN ATTORNEY WAKES UP FROM SURGERY AND ASKS WHY ALL THE SHADES ARE DRAWN.

THE DOCTOR ANSWERS, "THERE IS A FIRE ACROSS THE STREET. WE DIDN'T WANT YOU TO THINK YOU HAD DIED!"

JOKE 50

Q: WHAT DID THE JUDGE'S SON DO TO HER WHEN HE GOT ARRESTED?

A: HE EMBARISTER.

JOKE 51

Q: HAVE YOU HEARD? THE NRA FILED FOR BANKRUPTCY!

A: NO WAY, I THOUGHT THEY WERE LOADED!

JOKE 52

Q: WHAT DO YOU CALL AN ATTORNEY WITH AN IQ OF 50?

A: YOUR HONOR.

JOKE 53

Q: A LEPRECHAUN, THE EASTER BUNNY, AN HONEST LAWYER, AND AN OLD DRUNK SIMULTANEOUSLY SPOT A GOLD COIN. WHO GETS IT?

A: THE OLD DRUNK OF COURSE! THE OTHERS ARE IMAGINARY CREATURES.

JOKE 54

Q: WHAT DO YOU CALL THOUSANDS OF LAWYERS AT THE BOTTOM OF THE OCEAN?

A: THE GREAT BARRISTER REEF.

JOKE 55

Q: HOW MANY ATTORNEYS DOES IT TAKE TO TILE A FLOOR?

A: DEPENDS ON HOW THIN YOU SLICE THEM

JOKE 56

Q: HOW MANY ATTORNEY JOKES ARE THERE?

A: ONLY A FEW. THE REST ARE TRUE STORIES.

JOKE 57

Q: WHAT IS SOMETHING SWANS CAN DO, DUCKS CAN'T DO, AND LAWYERS SHOULD DO?

A: SHOVE THEIR BILLS UP THEIR ASSES.

JOKE 58

Q: HOW CAN YOU TELL THE DIFFERENCE BETWEEN A LAWYER AND A VULTURE?

A: LAWYERS RACK UP FREQUENT FLYER MILES.

JOKE 59

Q: WHAT IS THE DIFFERENCE BETWEEN A BOXING REFEREE AND AN ATTORNEY?

A: THE REFEREE DOESN'T GET PAID MORE FOR A LONGER FIGHT.

JOKE 60

Q: WHERE DID DRACULA LEARN TO SUCK PEOPLE DRY?

A: LAW SCHOOL.

JOKE 61

Q: WHAT DO JUDGES PUT IN THEIR DRINKS?

A: JUST ICE.

JOKE 62

Q: WHAT HAPPENS WHEN YOU CROSS AN ATTORNEY WITH THE GODFATHER?

A: YOU END UP WITH AN OFFER YOU CAN'T UNDERSTAND.

JOKE 63

Q: WHAT HAPPENED TO THE THIEF WHO STOLE THE PUNCTUATION KEYS FROM THE JUDGE'S KEYBOARD?

A: THEY GOT A LONG SENTENCE.

JOKE 64

PSA: THE POST OFFICE WILL NO LONGER MAKE STAMPS WITH PICTURES OF LAWYERS ON THEM. PEOPLE CAN'T FIGURE OUT WHICH SIDE TO SPIT ON.

JOKE 65

Q: WHAT'S THE DIFFERENCE BETWEEN AN ATTORNEY AND A TICK?

A: THE TICK FALLS OFF WHEN YOU DIE.

JOKE 66

Q: WHY ARE LAWYERS TERRIBLE TO DATE?

A: THEY LIE STILL.

JOKE 67

JESUS ENTERED A COURTROOM.

THERE WAS A MAN WHO COULD NOT WALK.

JESUS ASKED HIM, "HAVE YOU BEEN INJURED IN AN ACCIDENT THAT WAS NOT YOUR FAULT?"

JOKE 68

Q: HOW DO LAWYERS SNEAK SNACKS INTO COURT?

A: IN THEIR BRIEFS.

JOKE 69

Q: WHY DON'T LAWYERS LIKE SPRING MORNINGS?

A: WAY TOO MUCH DEW PROCESS.

JOKE 70

Q: WHY DID GOD MAKE COCKROACHES BEFORE LAWYERS?

A: HE NEEDED PRACTICE.

JOKE 71

THERE ARE TWO TYPES OF ATTORNEYS.

THOSE WHO KNOW THE LAW, AND THOSE WHO KNOW THE JUDGE!

JOKE 72

DOCTOR: MA'AM, I HAVE SOME BAD NEWS. YOU ONLY HAVE 3 MONTHS TO LIVE.

PATIENT: THAT'S AWFUL! IS THERE ANYTHING THAT I CAN DO?

DOCTOR: THERE IS ONE THING... YOU COULD MARRY AN ATTORNEY...

PATIENT: WILL THAT HELP ME LIVE LONGER?

DOCTOR: NOT AT ALL, BUT IT WILL ABSOLUTELY FEEL LIKE IT!

HEY GIRL,
WHEN I THINK ABOUT
YOU, I BECOME FULLY
VESTED.

Q: WHAT'S THE
DIFFERENCE BETWEEN
A GIGOLO AND AN
ATTORNEY?

A: A GIGOLO ONLY
SCREWS ONE CLIENT AT
A TIME.

JOKE 75

"I DON'T THINK YOU CAN MAKE A LAWYER HONEST BY AN ACT OF LEGISLATURE. YOU'VE GOT TO WORK ON HIS CONSCIENCE. AND HIS LACK OF CONSCIENCE IS WHAT MAKES HIM A LAWYER."

– WILL ROGERS

JOKE 76

Q: HAVE YOU HEARD ABOUT THE ATTORNEY WHO SUED THE COFFIN COMPANY?

A: IT WAS AN OPEN AND SHUT CASE.

JOKE 77

Q: WHAT DO LAWYERS HAVE IN COMMON WITH SPERM?

A: ONE OUT OF MILLIONS HAS A CHANCE OF BECOMING HUMAN.

JOKE 78

Q: HAVE YOU HEARD ABOUT THE PERSONAL INJURY LAWYER THAT GOT IN A CAR ACCIDENT?

A: YEAH, THE AMBULANCE HE WAS CHASING STOPPED UNEXPECTEDLY.

JOKE 79

Q: WHAT IS THE PROBLEM WITH JOKES ABOUT LAWYERS?

A: LAWYERS DON'T FIND THEM FUNNY. NOBODY ELSE THINKS THEY'RE JOKES.

JOKE 80

Q: HOW DOES AN ATTORNEY SAY "F*%$ YOU"?

A: "TRUST ME."

JOKE 81

HEY GIRL,
I'D HAVE TO PLEAD
INSANITY IF I EVER
LEFT YOU.

JOKE 82

Q: DO YOU KNOW
THE DIFFERENCE
BETWEEN A LADY
LAWYER AND A
PITBULL?

A: LIPSTICK.

JOKE 83

CLIENT: IS IT A CRIME TO THROW SODIUM CHLORIDE AT SOMEONE?

LAWYER: OF COURSE! THAT'S ASSAULT!

CLIENT: OK, I KNOW IT'S A SALT... BUT IS IT A CRIME?

JOKE 84

"LAWYERS ARE LIKE RHINOCEROSES: THICK-SKINNED, SHORT-SIGHTED, AND ALWAYS READY TO CHARGE."

— DAVID MELLOR

Q: HOW MANY ATTORNEYS DOES IT TAKE TO SCREW IN A LIGHT BULB?

A: ONE. HE JUST HOLDS THE LIGHT BULB IN PLACE AND THE REST OF THE WORLD REVOLVES AROUND HIM!

CLIENT: I GOT A PUPPY FOR MY SON.

LAWYER: GOOD TRADE.

JOKE 87

Q: WHAT'S THE DIFFERENCE BETWEEN AN ATTORNEY AND A BOA CONSTRICTOR?

A: EVENTUALLY, THE SNAKE WILL LET GO.

JOKE 88

JUDGE: STATE YOUR NAME.

MAN: NOT GUILTY.

JUDGE: EXCUSE ME?

MAN: FIRST NAME NOT. LAST NAME GUILTY. I HAD IT LEGALLY CHANGED.

JUDGE: SO, YOU ARE NOT GUILTY?

MAN: *WALKS OUT A FREE MAN*

JOKE 89

Q: WHAT'S THE DIFFERENCE BETWEEN VULTURES AND LAWYERS?

A: REMOVABLE WING TIPS.

JOKE 90

HEY GIRL,

ARE YOU INTO REVERSE BIFURCATION?

JOKE 91

Q: HOW DID THE ATTORNEY SWAY THE JUDGE?

A: THEY DROPPED THEIR BRIEFS.

JOKE 92

Q: WHAT'S THE DIFFERENCE BETWEEN A BIRD AND A BANKRUPT LAWYER?

A: A BIRD CAN STILL MAKE A DEPOSIT ON A BMW.

JOKE 93

GOD WAS FED UP WITH SATAN AND DECIDED TO TAKE HIM TO COURT.

SATAN WAS DELIGHTED. WHERE WAS GOD GOING TO FIND A LAWYER?!?

JOKE 94

LAWYER: ALL RESPONSES MUST BE ORAL, IS THAT CLEAR?

WITNESS: ORAL.

JOKE 95

"LAWYERS ARE JUST LIKE PHYSICIANS: WHAT ONE SAYS, THE OTHER CONTRADICTS."

— SHOLOM ALEICHEM

JOKE 96

Q: WHAT DO YOU CALL A LEGAL COFFEE EXPERT?

A: BARRISTA.

JOKE 97

Q: WHAT SHOULD YOU TOSS TO A DROWNING LAWYER?

A: HIS PARTNERS.

JOKE 98

Q: WHY IS IT AGAINST THE LAW FOR ATTORNEYS TO SLEEP WITH THEIR CLIENTS?

A: TO AVOID PEOPLE FROM GETTING CHARGED TWICE FOR THE SAME SERVICE.

JOKE 99

ONE WORTHLESS MAN IS A DISGRACE.

TWO ARE A LAW FIRM.

THREE OR MORE ARE CONGRESS!

JOKE 100

"YOU WIN SOME AND YOU LOSE SOME, BUT YOU GET PAID FOR ALL OF THEM."

– ANONYMOUS

JOKE 101

Q: WHAT IS THE DIFFERENCE BETWEEN A BUCKETFUL OF POND SCUM AND AN ATTORNEY?

A: THE BUCKET.

JOKE 102

Q: HOW ARE ATTORNEYS LIKE NUCLEAR WEAPONS?

A: IF ONE SIDE HAS ONE, THEN THE OTHER SIDE MUST GET ONE!

JOKE 103

Q: WHEN WAS COPPER WIRE FIRST INVENTED?

A: WHEN TWO LAWYERS FOUGHT OVER A PENNY.

JOKE 104

ARGUING WITH AN ATTORNEY IS LIKE WRESTLING WITH A PIG IN MUD.

EVENTUALLY YOU REALIZE THEY LIKE IT.

JOKE 105

AN EMBEZZLING MILLIONAIRE WENT TO AN ATTORNEY.

THE ATTORNEY TOLD HIM NOT TO WORRY, THAT HE WOULD NEVER BE ARRESTED WITH THAT MUCH MONEY.

IT WAS TRUE!

WHEN THE MAN WAS ARRESTED, HE DIDN'T HAVE A PENNY!

JOKE 106

Q: WHY ARE DEAD LAWYERS BURIED 10 FEET UNDER (INSTEAD OF ONLY 6?)

A: BECAUSE WAY DEEP DOWN, LAWYERS ARE GOOD PEOPLE TOO.

JOKE 107

AN ATTORNEY DIES AND GOES TO THE PEARLY GATES.

HE SPEAKS TO ST. PETER AND SAYS, "THERE MUST BE A MISTAKE, I'M ONLY 48!"

"48?" SAYS ST. PETER, "NO, ACCORDING TO OUR CALCULATIONS YOU ARE 85.... WE REFERENCED YOUR TIME SHEETS."

JOKE 108

"A LAWYER WILL DO ANYTHING TO WIN A CASE, SOMETIMES HE WILL EVEN TELL THE TRUTH."

- PATRICK MURRAY

Q: DOCTORS TAKE HIPPOCRATIC OATHS. WHAT DO LAWYERS TAKE?

A: HYPOCRITICAL OATHS.

HEY GIRL, WANT TO SEE MY MENS REA?

JOKE 111

Q: WHAT DO YOU CALL A BAD ATTORNEY?

A: SENATOR.

JOKE 112

LAWYER: DOCTOR, HOW MANY OF YOUR AUTOPSIES HAVE YOU PERFORMED ON DEAD PEOPLE?

WITNESS: ALL OF THEM! IF THEY ARE ALIVE, THEY PUT UP TOO MUCH OF A FIGHT!

JOKE 113

Q: WHAT DO LAWYERS USE TO HELP THEM SEE WHEN THEY HAVE TROUBLE READING SMALL PRINT?

A: CONTRACT LENSES.

JOKE 114

Q: WHAT HAPPENS WHEN YOU CROSS A CROOKED ATTORNEY WITH A BAD POLITICIAN?

A: CHELSEA CLINTON.

JOKE 115

Q: WHAT'S THE DIFFERENCE BETWEEN A LAWYER AND A PARASITIC TAPE WORM?

A: EVENTUALLY YOU CAN GET RID OF A TAPEWORM.

JOKE 116

LAWYER: ARE YOU MARRIED?

WITNESS: NOT ANYMORE, I'M DIVORCED.

LAWYER: WHAT DID YOUR PARTNER DO BEFORE THE DIVORCE?

WITNESS: LOTS OF THINGS I DIDN'T KNOW ABOUT!

JOKE 117

Q: WHAT'S THE DIFFERENCE BETWEEN A HERD OF CATTLE AND A LAWYER?

A: THE LAWYER CHARGES MORE.

JOKE 118

HEY GIRL,

THERE IS NO BURDEN OF PROOF FOR HOW SEXY YOU ARE.

JOKE 119

JARED FROM SUBWAY RECEIVED A 16-YEAR PRISON SENTENCE.

BUT HE DIDN'T CARE.

BECAUSE HE WAS FINE WITH ANYTHING UNDER 18.

JOKE 120

Q: WHAT DO YOU CALL A LAWYER WHO WORKS FOR SEXUAL FAVORS?

A: PRO-BONER.

JOKE 121

Q: WHAT DID THE PERSONAL INJURY LAWYER NAME HIS DAUGHTER?

A: SUE.

JOKE 122

BAILIFF: DO YOU SWEAR TO TELL THE TRUTH, THE WHOLE TRUTH, AND NOTHING BUT THE TRUTH?

ME: NO

JUDGE: THIS HAS NEVER HAPPENED BEFORE...

JOKE 123

Q: WHY WAS THE COURTROOM MASTURBATOR FOUND NOT GUILTY?

A: HE GOT OFF ON A TECHNICALITY.

JOKE 124

A JUDGE FROM NORTH KOREA WAS LAUGHING AS HE EXITED THE COURTROOM.

HIS FRIEND ASKED, "WHAT'S SO FUNNY?"

THE JUDGE REPLIED, "I JUST HEARD THE MOST HILARIOUS POLITICAL JOKE!"

"TELL ME!" SAYS THE FRIEND.

"OH, I CAN'T! I JUST SENT SOMEONE TO PRISON FOR IT!"

JOKE 125

WHERE THERE'S A WILL, THERE ARE DOZENS OF RELATIVES.

JOKE 126

Q: HOW CAN YOU TELL THE DIFFERENCE BETWEEN A LAWYER AND A SEA SLUG?

A: ONE IS A SPINELESS, DISGUSTING BLOB. THE OTHER IS A SEA CREATURE.

THIS JUDGE IS KNOWN FOR SLAMMING HIS GAVEL AND YELLING "GUILTY!" DURING OPENING ARGUMENTS.

HE CLEARLY STRUGGLES WITH PREMATURE ADJUDICATION.

Q: WHAT DO YOU CALL SANTA CLAUS AFTER HE DECLARES BANKRUPTCY?

A: ST. NICKELESS.

JOKE 129

Q: HOW COME CALIFORNIA HAS THE MOST LAWYERS IN THE USA AND NEW JERSEY HAS THE HIGHEST NUMBER OF TOXIC WASTE SITES?

A: NJ GOT THE FIRST CHOICE.

JOKE 130

Q: WHAT DO YOU CALL A DOZEN SKYDIVING ATTORNEYS?

A: SKEET.

JOKE 131

Q: HOW MANY ATTORNEYS DOES IT TAKE TO SCREW IN A LIGHTBULB?

A: HOW MANY CAN YOU AFFORD?

JOKE 132

"I BUSTED A MIRROR AND GOT SEVEN YEARS BAD LUCK, BUT MY LAWYER THINKS HE CAN GET ME FIVE."

– STEPHEN WRIGHT

JOKE 133

Q: HOW CAN YOU TELL THE DIFFERENCE BETWEEN AN ONION AND A LAWYER?

A: MOST PEOPLE CRY WHEN THEY CUT UP AN ONION.

JOKE 134

Q: HOW DO ATTORNEYS SAY GOODBYE?

A: "WE'LL BE SUING YOU!"

BONUS JOKES TO
ENTERTAIN YOUR
CLIENTS

BONUS JOKE 1

Q: WHAT HAPPENED WHEN THE GRAPE GOT SQUISHED?

A: HE LET OUT A LITTLE WINE.

BONUS JOKE 2

I AM JUST SO GOOD AT SLEEPING.

I CAN DO IT WITH MY EYES CLOSED!

BONUS JOKE 3

Q: WHAT KIND OF CAR DOES A CHICKEN DRIVE?

A: A YOLKSWAGEN.

BONUS JOKE 4

NAME A KIND OF WATER THAT CAN'T FREEZE.

HOT WATER.

BONUS JOKE 5

Q: WHAT DO SANTA'S ELVES LISTEN TO AS THEY WORK?

A: WRAP MUSIC.

BONUS JOKE 6

Q: WHEN IS A DOOR NOT REALLY A DOOR?

A: WHEN IT'S AJAR.

BONUS JOKE 7

Q: WHAT GETS WETTER THE MORE IT DRIES?

A: A TOWEL.

BONUS JOKE 8

I DON'T PLAY SOCCER BECAUSE I'M GOOD AT IT.

I JUST DO IT FOR THE KICKS.

BONUS JOKE 9

"MY WIFE SUFFERS FROM A SERIOUS DRINKING PROBLEM."

"IS SHE AN ALCOHOLIC?"

"NO, BUT I AM! BUT SHE IS THE ONE WHO SUFFERS!"

BONUS JOKE 10

I AM ONLY FAMILIAR WITH 25/26 LETTERS OF THE ALPHABET.

I DO NOT KNOW WHY.

BONUS JOKE 11

Q: WHY DID THE WORKER GET FIRED FROM THE CRANBERRY JUICE FACTORY?

A: LACK OF CONCENTRATION.

BONUS JOKE 12

Q: WHY ARE ELEVATOR JOKES SO HILARIOUS?

A: THEY WORK ON SO MANY LEVELS.

BONUS JOKE 13

WOW SO MUCH HAS CHANGED SINCE MY GIRLFRIEND GOT PREGNANT.

FOR EXAMPLE- MY NAME, ADDRESS, AND PHONE NUMBER!

BONUS JOKE 14

Q: WHAT IS A LAZY PERSON'S FAVORITE EXERCISE?

A: DIDDLY SQUATS!

BONUS JOKE 15

Q: WHY WAS IT RUDE FOR A SNOWMAN TO PICK A CARROT?

A: BECAUSE HE WAS PICKING HIS NOSE!

BONUS JOKE 16

Q: WHAT DID THE PAPA CHIMNEY SAY TO THE BABY CHIMNEY?

A: YOU ARE TOO YOUNG TO BE SMOKING!

BONUS JOKE 17

Q: WHY WERE THE KITCHEN UTENSILS STUCK TOGETHER?

A: BECAUSE THEY WERE SPOONING.

BONUS JOKE 18

Q: WHAT IS THE BEST THING TO DO WHEN YOU SEE A SPACEMAN?

A: PARK IN IT!

BONUS JOKE 19

Q: WHY DO GHOSTS RIDE IN ELEVATORS?

A: BECAUSE IT LIFTS THEIR SPIRITS.

BONUS JOKE 20

Q: WHAT DOES IT SOUND LIKE WHEN A COW BREAKS THE SOUND BARRIER?

A: COW-BOOM!

BONUS JOKE 21

Q: WHERE DID THE COMPUTER GO DANCING?

A: THE DISC-O!

BONUS JOKE 22

Q: WHY WAS 6 AFRAID OF 7?

A: BECAUSE 7-8-9.

BONUS JOKE 23

DON'T WORRY, YOU
AREN'T COMPLETELY
USELESS.

YOU CAN ALWAYS SERVE
AS A BAD EXAMPLE.

BONUS JOKE 24

Q: WHAT IS THE BEST WAY
TO WATCH A FLY-FISHING
TOURNAMENT?

A: LIVE STREAM.

BONUS JOKE 25

DAUGHTER: DAD, I'M HUNGRY!

DAD: HI HUNGRY, I'M DAD.

BONUS JOKE 26

Q: WHY DID THE JELLYBEAN WANT TO GO TO SCHOOL?

A: TO BECOME A SMARTIE.

BONUS JOKE 27

Q: WHAT DID THE BASEBALL CAP SAY TO THE SOMBRERO?

A: YOU STAY HERE, I'LL GO ON AHEAD.

BONUS JOKE 28

Q: WHAT KINDS OF PICTURES DO OYSTERS TAKE?

A: SHELLFIES.

BONUS JOKE 29

Q: HOW DO YOU KEEP A BAGEL FROM RUNNING AWAY?

A: LOX IT UP.

BONUS JOKE 30

Q: WHERE DO COWS GO ON A DATE?

A: THE MOO-VIES.

BONUS JOKE 31

Q: WHAT HAPPENS WHEN A FROG'S TRUCK DIES?

A: HE GETS A JUMP. AND IF THAT DOESN'T WORK, HE HAS TO GET TOAD.

BONUS JOKE 32

Q: DO YOU KNOW THE BEST WAY TO MAKE SOMEONE CURIOUS?

A: I'LL TELL YOU TOMORROW!

BONUS JOKE 33

Q: WHY ARE DOGS SUCH BAD STORYTELLERS?

A: BECAUSE THEY ONLY HAVE ONE TALE.

BONUS JOKE 34

Q: WHY WAS THE NOSE MAD AT THE FINGER?

A: BECAUSE HE WAS ALWAYS PICKING ON HIM!

BONUS JOKE 35

Q: HOW CAN YOU STOP AN ASTRONAUT'S BABY FROM CRYING?

A: YOU JUST ROCKET!

BONUS JOKE 36

Q: WHAT DO YOU CALL A MOUNTAIN WHO WANTS TO BE A COMEDIAN?

A: HILL-ARIOUS.

BONUS JOKE 37

Q: WHAT IS A TORNADO'S FAVORITE GAME?

A: TWISTER!

BONUS JOKE 38

Q: I HAVE EIGHTEEN EYES, TWENTY TEETH, AND A VERY LONG NOSE. WHAT AM I?

A: UGLY.

BONUS JOKE 39

Q: HOW DO YOU MAKE A TISSUE DANCE?

A: PUT A LITTLE BOOGIE IN IT!

BONUS JOKE 40

Q: WHAT DO YOU CALL A FLOWER THAN RUNS ON ELECTRICITY?

A: A POWER PLANT.

BONUS JOKE 41

Q: WHY IS IT DIFFICULT TO EXPLAIN JOKES TO KLEPTOMANIACS?

A: BECAUSE THEY ARE ALWAYS TAKING THINGS, LITERALLY.

BONUS JOKE 42

Q: WHY CAN'T YOU HEAR A PTERODACTYL USING THE BATHROOM?

A: BECAUSE THE 'P' IS SILENT.

BONUS JOKE 43

I WAS TOLD I SHOULD WRITE A BOOK.

WHAT A NOVEL CONCEPT.

BONUS JOKE 44

Q: WHAT TIME DID THE DAD GO TO THE DENTIST?

A: TOOTH HURT-y.

BONUS JOKE 45

Q: DO YOU KNOW HOW POPULAR THAT CEMETERY IS?

A: PEOPLE ARE JUST DYING TO GET IN THERE!

BONUS JOKE 46

Q: WHAT KIND OF TREE FITS IN YOUR HAND?

A: A PALM TREE!

BONUS JOKE 47

Q: WHAT DID THE TONSIL SAY TO THE ADENOID?

A: GET DRESSED, THE DOCTOR IS TAKING US OUT!

BONUS JOKE 48

Q: WHERE DO BABY CATS LEARN HOW TO SWIM?

A: THE KITTY POOL.

BONUS JOKE 49

Q: WHAT IS THE BEST PRESENT EVER?

A: A BUSTED DRUM. YOU CAN'T BEAT IT!

BONUS JOKE 50

I WAS FIRED FROM THE BANK TODAY.

A WOMAN ASKED ME TO CHECK HER BALANCE, SO I PUSHED HER OVER.

BONUS JOKE 51

Q: WHEN DOES A JOKE BECOME A DAD JOKE?

A: WHEN IT BECOMES APPARENT.

BONUS JOKE 52

Q: WHY DID THE PAPER TOWEL ROLL DOWNHILL?

A: TO GET TO THE BOTTOM.

BONUS JOKE 53

Q: WHAT DID ONE DORITO FARMER SAY TO THE OTHER?

A: COOL RANCH!

BONUS JOKE 54

Q: WHY DON'T GHOSTS GO TRICK OR TREATING?

A: BECAUSE THEY HAVE NO BODY TO GO WITH.

BONUS JOKE 55

Q: WHICH DAY DO CHICKENS DREAD?

A: FRI-DAY.

BONUS JOKE 56

Q: WHY DID THE WOMAN GET FIRED FROM THE CALENDAR FACTORY?

A: BECAUSE SHE TOOK A FEW DAYS OFF.

BONUS JOKE 57

Q: CAN A GRASSHOPPER JUMP HIGHER THAN A HOUSE?

A: OF COURSE! HOUSES CAN'T JUMP.

BONUS JOKE 58

ONE COMPANY OWNER IS TALKING WITH ANOTHER.

"HOW DO YOU GET ALL OF YOUR EMPLOYEES TO WORK ON TIME?"

"IT'S EASY! 40 EMPLOYEES, 30 PARKING SPACES!"

BONUS JOKE 59

GYM TEACHER'S FAMOUS LAST WORD:

"ALL SPEARS TO ME!"

BONUS JOKE 60

Q: HOW MANY APPLES GROW ON A TREE?

A: ALL OF THEM.

BONUS JOKE 61

CUSTOMER: I AM OUTRAGED! THERE IS A HAIR IN MY SOUP!

WAITER: AT THIS PRICE, WHAT DID YOU EXPECT? A WHOLE WIG?

BONUS JOKE 62

Q: WHERE DID THE NEWLYWED BUNNIES GO AFTER THEIR WEDDING?

A: ON A BUNNY-MOON!

BONUS JOKE 63

Q: WHY DID THE BANK GET BORED?

A: BECAUSE IT LOST INTEREST.

BONUS JOKE 64

SON: DAD, WHAT IS AN ALCOHOLIC?

DAD: DO YOU SEE THOSE 4 TREES? AN ALCOHOLIC WOULD SEE 8.

SON: BUT THERE ARE ONLY 2 TREES.

BONUS JOKE 65

I HAVE A SERIOUS ELEVATOR PHOBIA.

SO, I TAKE STEPS TO AVOID THEM.

BONUS JOKE 66

Q: WHAT DO YOU CALL A FIBBING KITTY?

A: FELINE.

BONUS JOKE 67

Q: WHAT IS INVISIBLE AND SMELLS LIKE WORMS?

A: A BIRD'S FART.

BONUS JOKE 68

DOCTOR: YOUR TEST RESULTS SHOW THAT YOU WILL LIVE TO BE 70.

PATIENT: BUT I JUST TURNED 70.

DOCTOR: I KNOW, I TOLD YOU TO TAKE BETTER CARE OF YOURSELF!

BONUS JOKE 69

Q: WHY SHOULD YOU AVOID EATING A WATCH?

A: BECAUSE IT'S TOO TIME CONSUMING.

BONUS JOKE 70

Q: WHAT IS THE MOST PATRIOTIC SPORT?

A: FLAG FOOTBALL.

BONUS JOKE 71

Q: WHY DID THE BICYCLE FALL ASLEEP?

A: IT WAS TWO-TIRED.

BONUS JOKE 72

Q: HAVE YOU HEARD ABOUT CORDUROY PILLOWS?

A: THEY ARE MAKING HEADLINES.

BONUS JOKE 73

Q: HAVE YOU HEARD ABOUT THE NAKED WOMAN WHO ROBS BANKS?

A: NOBODY CAN REMEMBER HER FACE!

BONUS JOKE 74

Q: HOW DO YOU KNOW IF THERE IS AN ELEPHANT UNDER YOUR BED?

A: YOUR HEAD HITS THE CEILING!

BONUS JOKE 75

Q: WHAT TIME IS IT WHEN A CLOCK STRIKES 13?

A: TIME TO GET A NEW CLOCK!

BONUS JOKE 76

Q: WHAT DOES A BABY COMPUTER CALL ITS FATHER?

A: DATA.

BONUS JOKE 77

Q: WHY WAS THE ALGEBRA BOOK DEPRESSED?

A: IT WAS FULL OF PROBLEMS.

BONUS JOKE 78

Q: WHAT DID THE PILLOW SAY WHEN IT FELL OFF THE BED?

A: OH SHEET!

BONUS JOKE 79

Q: WHAT DO YOU CALL A DROID THAT TAKES THE SCENIC ROUTE?

A: R2 DETOUR.

BONUS JOKE 80

Q: WHAT DO YOU CALL A MINIATURE PONY WITH A SORE THROAT?

A: A LITTLE HOARSE.

BONUS JOKE 81

Q: WHAT DO YOU CALL A BLIND DINOSAUR?

A: A DO-YOU-THINK-HE-SAW-US.

BONUS JOKE 82

Q: HOW DOES AN ESKIMO BUILD A HOUSE?

A: IGLOOS IT TOGETHER.

BONUS JOKE 83

Q: WHY DID THE POLICEMAN SMEAR PEANUT BUTTER ON THE ROAD?

A: TO GO WITH THE TRAFFIC JAM!

BONUS JOKE 84

Q: WHY ARE DOCTORS SO CALM?

A: BECAUSE THEY HAVE A LOT OF PATIENTS.

BONUS JOKE 85

Q: WHAT KIND OF MUSIC DO ALIENS LISTEN TO?

A: NEP-TUNES.

BONUS JOKE 86

ONCE I MET A GIRL WHO HAD 12 NIPPLES.

SOUNDS FREAKY, DOZEN TIT.

BONUS JOKE 87

IF A TODDLER REFUSES TO GO TO SLEEP, ARE THEY GUILTY OF RESISTING A REST?

BONUS JOKE 88

Q: WHAT DID THE BABY CORN SAY WHEN HIS DAD WENT TO WORK?

A: WHERE IS POPCORN?

BONUS JOKE 89

Q: WHY ARE BASKETBALL PLAYERS DIFFICULT TO DINE WITH?

A: BECAUSE THEY ARE CONSTANTLY DRIBBLING.

BONUS JOKE 90

YESTERDAY MY WIFE ASKED ME FOR SOME LIPSTICK.

I ACCIDENTLY GAVE HER A GLUE STICK AND SHE STILL ISN'T TALKING TO ME.

BONUS JOKE 91

Q: WHAT DO YOU CALL AN INCREDIBLY OLD SNOWMAN?

A: WATER.

BONUS JOKE 92

DOCTOR: HELLO. DO YOU HAVE AN EYE PROBLEM?

PATIENT: WOW! YES, HOW DID YOU KNOW?

DOCTOR: WELL YOU CAME IN THROUGH THE WINDOW INSTEAD OF THE DOOR.

BONUS JOKE 93

Q: WHY DO FISH LIVE IN SALT WATER?

A: BECAUSE PEPPER MAKES THEM SNEEZE!

BONUS JOKE 94

I USED TO HATE FACIAL HAIR.

BUT THEN IT GREW ON ME.

BONUS JOKE 95

Q: WHAT DID THE FISHERMAN SAY WHEN HE ATE THE CLOWNFISH?

A: THAT TASTED A LITTLE FUNNY.

BONUS JOKE 96

Q: WHY DID THE CHIMPANZEE FALL OUT OF THE TREE?

A: IT WAS DEAD.

BONUS JOKE 97

A FAMISHED TERMITE WALKS INTO A BAR.

HE SAYS, "WHERE IS THE BAR TENDER?"

BONUS JOKE 98

Q: WHY ARE GHOSTS THE WORST LIARS?

A: BECAUSE YOU CAN SEE RIGHT THROUGH THEM.

BONUS JOKE 99

Q: WHAT DID THE MOUNTAIN SAY TO THE BLUFF?

A: HEY CLIFF!

BONUS JOKE 100

Q: WHAT DO YOU CALL AN AMERICAN BEE?

A: A USB.

BONUS JOKE 101

Q: WHY CAN'T A HAND BE 12 INCHES LONG?

A: BECAUSE THEN IT WOULD BE A FOOT.

BONUS JOKE 102

Q: WHAT DID THE PLATE SAY TO THE CUP?

A: DINNER IS ON ME!

BONUS JOKE 103

WHOEVER INVENTED AUTOCORRECT IS A MASSHOLE.

HE CAN DUCK RIGHT OFF.

BONUS JOKE 104

Q: HAVE YOU HEARD ABOUT THE MAN WHO INVENTED THE KNOCK KNOCK JOKE?

A: HE WAS GIVEN THE NO-BELL PRIZE.

BONUS JOKE 105

Q: WHAT IS GREEN, POPULAR, AND SINGS?

A: ELVIS PARSLEY.

BONUS JOKE 106

Q: WHY IS 288 NEVER MENTIONED?

A: IT'S TWO GROSS.

BONUS JOKE 107

Q: WHAT KIND OF SHOES DO NINJAS WEAR?

A: SNEAKERS.

BONUS JOKE 108

Q: WHAT DO YOU CALL QUESO THAT DOESN'T BELONG TO YOU?

A: NACHO CHEESE.

BONUS JOKE 109

Q: WHAT IS THE BEST WAY TO IMPRESS A SQUIRREL?

A: ACT LIKE A NUT.